DK SUPER World

AUSTRALIA

Head down under to explore Australia's wealth
of wildlife, natural wonders, and lively cities

DK Learning

PRODUCED FOR DK BY

Editorial Caroline Wakeman Literary Agency
Design Collaborate Agency
Graphic Story Illustrator Matt Garbutt

Senior Editor Amelia Jones
Senior Art Editor Gilda Pacitti
Managing Editor Katherine Neep
Managing Art Editor Sarah Corcoran
Production Editor Andy Hilliard
Production Controller Rebecca Parton
Publisher Sarah Forbes
Managing Director, Learning Hilary Fine

First American Edition, 2025
Published in the United States by DK Publishing,
a division of Penguin Random House LLC
1745 Broadway, 20th Floor, New York, NY 10019

Copyright © 2025 Dorling Kindersley Limited
25 26 27 28 29 10 9 8 7 6 5 4 3 2 1
001–345902–Jul/2025

All rights reserved.
Without limiting the rights under the copyright reserved above, no part of this publication may be reproduced, stored in or introduced into a retrieval system, or transmitted, in any form, or by any means (electronic, mechanical, photocopying, recording, or otherwise), without the prior written permission of the copyright owner.

Published in Great Britain by Dorling Kindersley Limited

A catalog record for this book is
available from the Library of Congress.
HC ISBN: 978-0-5939-6655-6
PB ISBN: 978-0-5939-6654-9

DK books are available at special discounts when purchased in bulk for sales promotions, premiums, fund-raising, or educational use.
For details, contact: DK Publishing Special Markets,
1745 Broadway, 20th Floor, New York, NY 10019
SpecialSales@dk.com

Printed and bound in China

www.dk.com

This book was made with Forest Stewardship Council™ certified paper – one small step in DK's commitment to a sustainable future.
Learn more at www.dk.com/uk/information/sustainability

CONTENTS

MAP   4
Australia

FACT FILE   6
All About Australia

TERRAINS   8
Deserts, Reefs, and Beaches

LANDMARKS   10
Uluru

FLORA AND FAUNA   12
Wildlife Down Under

CULTURE   18
Diversity, Outdoor Pursuits, and Sports

RELIGION   22
Christianity and Spirituality

NATIONAL HOLIDAYS AND FESTIVALS   24
Outdoor Festivities

FOOD AND DRINK   26
Aussie Tucker

RECIPE   28
Anzac Biscuits

HOME, WORK, AND SCHOOL   30
Living, Learning, and Working

SCHOOL DAY DIARY   32
Charlie's Day

HISTORY   36
Terra Australis Incognita

THE MAN FROM SNOWY RIVER   38

VOCABULARY BUILDER   42
Saving the Koalas

GLOSSARY   44

INDEX   46

Words in **bold** are explained in the glossary on page 44.

AUSTRALIA

Australia is the only country in the world that covers a whole **continent**. It is in the Southern **Hemisphere**, which means it is south of the **equator**—it is sometimes known as "down under." Australia is famous for a unique area of land known as the outback: a mostly **arid** region that few people live in, which covers about 80 percent of the country.

FASCINATING FACT!

The longest fence in the world stretches more than 3,480 miles (5,600 km) from the east coast of Australia to the middle of the south coast. It was built to protect livestock and crops in the fertile regions of the southeast from dingoes and rabbits.

FACT FILE

ALL ABOUT AUSTRALIA

Australian National Flag

⚑ Flags: Australian National Flag, Australian Aboriginal Flag, Torres Strait Islander Flag

📍 Capital city: Canberra

👤 Population: Approx. 27 million

💬 Official language: English

💵 Currency: Australian dollar $

❀ National flower: Golden wattle

🐾 National animal: Red kangaroo

● National stone: Opal

🎵 National anthem: "Advance Australia Fair"

☆ Major exports: Wool, coal, gold

Flags

Australia has three flags. The Australian National Flag is the official flag for Australia as a country.

This flag represents the Aboriginal peoples. The red represents the Earth, the yellow the Sun, and the black represents the people, as well as a clay called ochre that's important to Aboriginal culture.

This flag represents the **Indigenous** peoples of the Torres Strait Islands. The blue is the sea, the green is the Earth, and the white design is a *dhari*: a headdress worn for dances.

FASCINATING FACT!

Opals are precious stones that **refract** light, giving them an ever-changing rainbow effect. More than 90 percent of the world's opals come from Australia.

Parliament House, Canberra

Capital city

Canberra is where Australia's government is based. It was built in 1913. There was an international competition to decide who would design the city, and American architects Walter Burley Griffin and Marion Mahony Griffin won.

FIND OUT!

Australia is its own continent, but it is also grouped with the surrounding islands, like New Zealand and Polynesia, using another name. Do you know what it is?

Answer: Oceania

TERRAINS

DESERTS, REEFS, AND BEACHES

Australia is famous for its desert terrains and long sandy beaches, but its landscapes are rich and varied. The southeast has lush rainforests and fertile land, and off the northeast coast is a gigantic coral reef. There are also some underground surprises.

Coral

Coral reefs
The Great Barrier Reef is the largest coral system in the world. Reefs are enormously important to the planet. A quarter of all ocean life relies on coral reefs for food and shelter. Reefs are very vulnerable to pollution and temperature changes in the water and will turn white when stressed.

FASCINATING FACT!

Though they look like rocks, corals are actually animals. They are related to jellyfish and form a hard shell for protection.

Great Artesian Basin
This is an enormous underground well of freshwater. The Basin is an aquifer: a layer of sand or gravel where the spaces are filled with water. The water emerges through cracks in the surface and feeds into springs and rivers.

Arid outback
The central outback region contains 10 deserts. These can reach temperatures of 122°F (50°C)! The sand is red because the rocks contain a lot of iron, which rusts and turns red over time. There are also **tropical** grasslands in the north of the outback and **shrublands** throughout.

Coasts
Australia has long beaches of white sand and warm emerald water. The white sand comes from parrotfish that live in the coral reefs, who excrete it as a waste product. The coasts also have some awe-inspiring cliffs, such as the ones on the coastline of the Great Australian **Bight** in the south.

Rainforests
The eastern regions of Australia have luscious tropical rainforests. The largest is the Daintree Rainforest in the northeast. It is one of the oldest rainforests on Earth—estimated at 180 million years old.

LANDMARKS

ULURU

Uluru is one of the most iconic sights in Australia. It is a red **monolith** that juts out of the flat desert ground. It stands taller than the Eiffel Tower in Paris, France. Uluru is in Uluru-Kata Tjuta National Park, right in the middle of the country.

Sacred site

Uluru-Kata Tjuta National Park is the land of the Anangu. For the Anangu, Uluru is a sacred site that was formed by their creation **ancestors**. Uluru is central to Anangu beliefs and storytelling. Caves around Uluru contain Anangu rock art that is thousands of years old.

FASCINATING FACT!

Uluru started out gray and became red over time as iron in the rock rusted. Some of the caves are still gray inside.

Formation of Uluru

About 550 million years ago, rain flowed down sandy mountains and deposited sandstone in a huge fan shape. This fan flooded, and the weight of the water compressed the sandstone into a hard boulder. Two million years later, **tectonic activity** pushed the land, including the boulder, upward. The softer sandstone eroded away, leaving the hard mound of Uluru exposed.

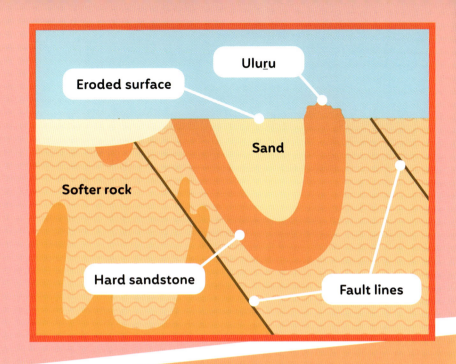

A brief history

In 1873, the Englishman William Gosse saw Uluru and named it Ayers Rock after an Australian politician. In 1958, it was made into a national park belonging to the government. The Anangu soon began efforts to get their land back. Finally, in 1985, they were given the deeds to the national park.

Conservation

The national park directors work with the Anangu to use traditional knowledge to manage fires, maintain water sources for animals and plants, and help plants to grow. With climate change, there is increased risk of **wildfires**, so fire management is very important.

FLORA AND FAUNA

WILDLIFE DOWN UNDER

Australia has more **endemic** wildlife than any other country in the world—80 percent of its plants, mammals, reptiles, and **amphibians** are found only in Australia. It is also the home of marsupials: a unique type of mammal who raise their young in a pouch on the front of their body.

MIGHTY MARSUPIALS

Red kangaroo
Kangaroos live in the outback regions. Their powerful legs allow them to jump more than 30 feet (9 m) in one go. They have long muscular tails that help to keep balance as they hop at speeds of up to 35 miles per hour (56 kph). Kangaroos also thump their tails against the ground to warn others of danger.

FASCINATING FACT!

When they're born, baby kangaroos (called joeys) are about the size of a bean. They immediately crawl into their mother's pouch to grow.

Koala
Koalas eat only from eucalyptus trees and will eat around 2.2 pounds (1 kg) of eucalyptus in a day. Eucalyptus is poisonous to most animals, but koalas have developed special stomachs to digest the leaves. Digesting poisonous leaves takes a lot of energy, so koalas sleep for 20 hours a day.

Tasmanian devil
These feisty marsupials have a loud throaty screech that they use when eating or under threat. They are **carnivorous** scavengers, vacuuming up any dead animal in the forest. On the **mainland**, they were hunted to extinction by dingoes. Now, they only exist on the island of Tasmania.

Wombat
Wombats live in large burrows that they dig with their powerful paws. Their pouches face backward so they don't fill up with soil. Their rumps are hard as rock to protect them from intruders. Wombats eat grasses and roots, and their poop is cube-shaped!

WOODLAND WILDLIFE

Laughing kookaburra
These kookaburras have a call that sounds a lot like laughter. The call is used to impress mates and warn of **predators**. They are carnivores and hunt snakes, frogs, and small mammals.

Eucalyptus
Also known as gum trees, these are the most common species of tree in Australia. Oils from eucalyptus have been used for medicines by Indigenous peoples for thousands of years. Eucalyptus flowers look spiky because they have no petals, only **stamen**.

Grey-headed flying fox
These are not foxes, but enormous bats. When open, their wings measure 3 feet (1 m) across. They are social creatures and spend their days in colonies of up to 200,000 bats. They love fruit, especially figs.

Cassowary
These big, flightless birds live in the forests of the northeast. They eat mostly fruit from the forest floor, which they dig up with their 4.5-inch (11.5 cm) claws. By digesting and excreting fruit seeds, they help trees grow.

AQUATIC ANIMALS

Platypus
Platypuses are one of only two types of mammals that lay eggs. They live in streams and rivers and hunt underwater by sensing electric pulses in their prey. Males have venomous spikes on their back legs and females produce milk in their sweat.

Box jellyfish
These are the most venomous creatures in the ocean. Box jellyfish use their tentacles to stun (or kill) their prey. The tentacles can grow up to 10 feet (3 m) long and have about 5,000 stingers each.

Giant clam
Giant clams live on the ocean floor and weigh about 440 pounds (200 kg). They are filter feeders, sucking in water and filtering for their food. A healthy giant clam can live to 100.

Mantis shrimp
These mighty **crustaceans** pack a punch. There are two types: spearers and punchers. Punchers punch through the shells of hard prey, like clams. Spearers strike soft prey, like worms and fish, with a spike on their arms.

ORGANISMS OF THE OUTBACK

Dingo
Australia's wild dogs roam the outback in packs of about 10. Unlike other dogs, they can rotate their wrist joints all the way round. This helps them to look backward to look for prey. It also means they can turn doorknobs and escape enclosures!

Golden wattle
Australia's national plant has bright yellow flowers like little puffs. These trees are incredibly resistant to drought and can grow in the barest lands of the outback. The trunks release a sap that hardens into a gum, which can be enjoyed as a sweet bush treat.

Emu
These flightless birds are **native** to Australia. Emus have huge territories over open plains and travel up to 15 miles (24 km) a day. The dark green emu eggs are sat on by their fathers for 55 days before they hatch.

Bonus bugs

Teddy bear bee

Rhinoceros beetle

Wolf spider

Blue ant

INVASIVE AND ENDANGERED SPECIES

Invasive rabbits
Europeans brought rabbits to Australia in the 1700s and they have been a problem ever since. They breed incredibly quickly and cause immense environmental damage by overgrazing, threatening native species. They also destroy crops, which causes **soil erosion**. There are about 200 million rabbits in Australia.

Rare regent honeyeaters
These vibrant birds are found in the forests of the southeast, where they drink nectar from eucalyptus trees. They can mimic the songs of other types of honeyeater birds. Land-clearing has destroyed much of their habitat, and they are considered critically endangered.

Endangered gliders
Greater gliders are tree-dwelling marsupials. They use flaps that stretch from their ankles to their elbows to glide through the air. They change direction using their tails like a rudder. In the last 20 years, their numbers have dropped by about 80 percent due to **deforestation** and wildfires.

CULTURE

DIVERSITY, OUTDOOR PURSUITS, AND SPORTS

Australia is a very ethnically mixed country. More than a quarter of people who live there were born in other countries. The Aboriginal peoples are the oldest living cultures on Earth. The abundance of open space and sunshine means people frequently enjoy the outdoors.

PEOPLE AND CUSTOMS

Diversity

An estimated half of Australians have European ancestry, and the main language spoken is English. There are around 984,000 Indigenous peoples and more than 250 Indigenous languages. There is also a huge Chinese community, and Mandarin is the second most-spoken language.

Australianisms

Australians like to abbreviate: "arvo" is afternoon, "mozzie" is mosquito, and "g'day" means good day. The common phrases "no worries" and "she'll be right" can mean both "don't worry about it" and "it will be OK." And if you're "flat out like a lizard drinking," you're working as hard as you can!

Aboriginal peoples

There are hundreds of Aboriginal **nations** and clans, each with their own languages, territories, practices, and stories. In Aboriginal culture, the connection between people and the **Country** is incredibly important. Many natural formations are considered sacred. Art is also important, and especially the use of ochre clay.

FASCINATING FACT!

The *yidaki*, or didgeridoo, is the oldest known instrument on Earth. Traditional Aboriginal didgeridoos are made from tree limbs that have been hollowed out by termites.

Torres Strait Islander peoples

These are the Indigenous peoples of the islands north of the mainland. There are five main nation groups with many individual communities. Their culture is a complex mix, with influences from Papua New Guinea, mainland Australia, and Asian islands further north. Dance, storytelling, cooking, and music are important cultural aspects.

OUTDOOR PURSUITS

Beach life
Three-quarters of Australians live within an hour of a beach. Many people spend free time playing frisbee, making sandcastles, swimming, or just relaxing in the sun. Going to the beach is so much a part of life that all beaches are legally available for anyone to use.

Barbecues
The barbecue, or "barbie," is a social event where people come together to enjoy food, sun, and company. Guests might tuck into a burger or some grilled shrimp and then play outdoor games like backyard cricket. Many parks have free barbecues for anyone to use.

Surfing
Australia is one of the top surfing destinations in the world. Surfers swim out into the ocean on a long board. When a wave comes, they hop up and ride the board back to shore. Surfing has become a whole culture in Australia, influencing clothes, movies, and music.

SPORTS

Cricket

Cricket is a bat-and-ball game played with two teams in a field. A batter and a bowler from different teams stand at either end of a strip called a pitch. The aim is to hit the ball and run as many lengths of the pitch as possible before you get out.

Bowler
Batter
Pitch

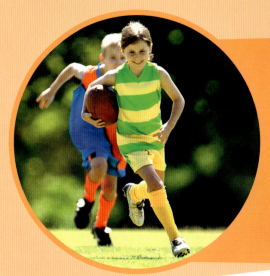

Australian rules football

Known as AFL, this is played in a field with two teams. Players try to get the oval-shaped ball to the other end of the field by passing it with their hands. To score, players kick the ball through two posts at the end. There are 36 players on a field at once.

Tennis

Australia hosts the Australian Open: an international tennis competition for top players. In tennis, two people (or two pairs of people) use a racket to hit a ball back and forth over a net until one of them misses. If your opponent misses, you score. But don't hit the ball outside the white lines, or your opponent scores!

RELIGION

CHRISTIANITY AND SPIRITUALITY

In Australia, just over 40 percent of people identify as Christian. Almost as many say they have no religion at all. After that, Islam, Hinduism, and Buddhism are the most common religions. Aboriginal and Torres Strait Islander groups have varied **belief systems**, and sometimes also follow Christianity.

St Mary's Cathedral, Sydney

Christianity

Christianity was brought to Australia by the Europeans. It is based on the teachings of Jesus Christ, who is believed by Christians to be the son of a single god. In Christian belief, Jesus teaches people to forgive others and treat people as they want to be treated. The Christian place of worship is a church or cathedral.

Tagai

Torres Strait Islander communities have individual beliefs and spiritual practices, united by a belief system known as Tagai. Tagai is also a constellation that guides people home. Stories tend to focus on the stars and the sea and their connection to the people. Many Torres Strait Islanders are Christian, too.

The Dreaming

This is a term for Aboriginal worldviews and beliefs. Stories describe how the universe was created, pass on cultural practices, and provide guidelines for how to live. Aboriginal sacred sites are places of nature, like mountains, lakes, and rock formations like Karlu Karlu.

Karlu Karlu

NATIONAL HOLIDAYS AND FESTIVALS

OUTDOOR FESTIVITIES

Australia's celebrations are often held outside in parks, beaches, and deserts. There are nine national holidays when schools and workplaces are closed across the country, but different states and cities have their own holidays too.

PUBLIC HOLIDAYS

Sandy snowman

Christmas
Christmas on December 25 is a Christian holiday, but it is celebrated by non-Christians too. In Australia, Christmas is in the middle of summer, so Australians often celebrate it on the beach or with a barbecue—or both!

Anzac Day
April 25 is a day of remembrance for people who fought in World War I. ANZAC stands for Australia and New Zealand Army Corps. Ceremonies are held, and people eat cookies made from oats, coconut, and syrup called "Anzac biscuits."

Regional days
Some holidays are specific to different regions of Australia. Canberra Day in March celebrates the naming of the city of Canberra. Southern Tasmania has Regatta Day in February, when a series of swimming and sports events are held. In Brisbane, a holiday is given in August so people can attend an **agricultural** fair called the Brisbane Exhibition (known as Ekka).

Parrtjima

This is a 10-day Aboriginal light festival. It takes place in April in the desert, where ancient Aboriginal cultures are celebrated with live music, art, performances, and colorful light installations. Here, the oldest cultures on Earth meet new technologies of art.

Floriade

This is a flower festival held in Canberra during September and October as a celebration of spring. More than a million flowers are in bloom in the Commonwealth Park. Each day there is a sensory hour: an hour without loud sounds so people can enjoy the flora in peace.

Moomba Festival

This festival is held in Melbourne over four days in March. It includes fairground rides, waterskiing events, fireworks, and a parade. There is also the Birdman Rally: a competition where people build small flying machines and try to glide over the river.

25

FOOD AND DRINK

AUSSIE TUCKER

Australian cuisine is influenced by local food availability, such as seafood and fresh fruits around the coasts. It also has touches of European **heritage**, such as savory meat pies from the United Kingdom and baked dishes from Italy, but with unique Aussie twists. "Grub" and "tucker" are Australian slang terms for food.

Meat pie
This Aussie classic is a small savory pie filled with meat and onions. People typically squirt a dollop of ketchup on top and eat it with their hands. Some prefer to take the pastry lid off, stir in ketchup, eat the filling with a spoon, then eat the pastry.

Meat pie

FASCINATING FACT!

A regional variation of this dish is the meat pie floater, where the pie is put in a bowl of thick pea soup.

Meat pie floater

Pavlova

This is the national dessert of Australia, made with a crisp meringue base covered in whipped cream and fruit. It was named after Russian ballerina Anna Pavlova, who toured Australia and New Zealand in the 1920s. Both countries claim it as their own invention.

Sodas

Passion fruit is a popular flavor of soda in Australia. Australians are also master brewers of ginger beer: a sweet soda with a spicy kick of ginger.

Chicken parmi

This adaptation of a classic Italian dish has become a comfort food staple in Australia. It is a breaded chicken cutlet in tomato sauce that's covered in cheese and then baked.

Smashed avo

This is simply mashed avocado on toast. Some say the Australians invented it. Smashed avo is usually eaten for breakfast or brunch, sometimes with tomatoes or eggs.

Here are some popular sweet treats:

Lamington
A sponge cake coated in chocolate and rolled in coconut flakes.

Fairy bread
Sliced white bread, buttered and covered in sprinkles.

Caramel slice
A cookie base with layers of caramel and chocolate.

Malted chocolate
A drink made from milk, chocolate, and malt powder.

RECIPE

ANZAC BISCUITS

This is a cookie made for Anzac Day in celebration of the soldiers who fought in World War I. In Australia, a cookie is called a biscuit. The original recipes did not include coconut, but it is now a common ingredient. It also gives the cookie a nice chew! This recipe makes 24 cookies to share with your friends or family.

Ingredients

- 1 ¼ cups (150 g) of all-purpose flour
- 1 cup (90 g) of rolled oats
- 1 cup (85 g) of desiccated coconut
- 1 cup (200 g) of granulated sugar
- 4 oz (120 g) of butter
- 2 tbsp. of light treacle or syrup
- ½ tsp. of baking soda

Method

1. First, prepare for baking. Pre-heat the oven to 350°F (180°C).
2. Line two baking trays with parchment paper (spread a little bit of butter in the corners underneath the paper to get it to stick).
3. Next, make the mixture. Get a big bowl. Add the flour, oats, coconut, and sugar, and stir it all together.
4. In a small saucepan, add the butter and treacle. Put it on a low heat and stir until the butter has melted.
5. Ask an adult to help you with this part: to the saucepan, add the baking soda and two tablespoons of hot water. The baking soda should make it foam up!
6. Carefully pour the liquid ingredients into the bowl of dry ingredients.
7. Gently stir it all together until it is well-mixed and sticky.
8. Now form the cookies. Use a tablespoon of mixture per cookie and roll it into a ball. Place each ball about an inch or two (2.5 to 5 cm) apart to give them space to spread out while they cook.
9. Bake for 12–15 minutes until they are golden in color. Let them cool before eating, then enjoy!

ADULT SUPERVISION REQUIRED

! Be careful not to eat too much sugar in a day. One Anzac biscuit is plenty.

Origins of the cookie

Anzac biscuits were originally given to soldiers as a long-lasting, easy-to-eat food that gave them a lot of energy. Oats are very nutritious and keep you full for a long time. The recipe purposefully doesn't use eggs because the cookies had to be transported on slow ships and eggs can go bad over time.

HOME, WORK, AND SCHOOL

LIVING, LEARNING, AND WORKING

Most of the population of Australia live in the south and east near the coasts, where temperatures are cooler. The outback covers about 80 percent of Australia, but less than 5 percent of the population live there. Of the people who do live in remote regions, it is estimated that half are Indigenous.

Keeping cool

Houses in Australia tend to have a lot of outdoor space, like verandas and gardens. Many homes are open plan so that air can flow through and keep the house cool. The north is hotter, so houses there have to be well-ventilated and are often air-conditioned.

Going to school

Children start primary school at age 5 or 6 and usually go to secondary school around age 12 (this can be a little bit different in some regions). School is compulsory until grade 10, and then for two more years students can choose to:
- Stay in school
- Do some training in a job
- Be in employment full-time

Or a combination of all three.

Primary school: grades 1–6

Secondary school: grades 7–10

Outdoor work

Mining is a huge industry in Australia. It is one of the world's largest producers of iron, lead, and gold—and opals! Australia is also one of the largest producers of wool. There are two-and-a-half times as many sheep as there are people.

Taking care

One of the fastest growing sectors is the healthcare and social care industry. One in every seven employed people in Australia work in this sector, as nurses, doctors, dentists, and ambulance drivers, but also as child carers, social workers, care home workers, and much more.

FASCINATING FACT!

There is a national service called the Royal Flying Doctor Service that flies doctors out to remote areas where people don't have access to healthcare.

SCHOOL DAY DIARY

CHARLIE'S DAY

Name: Charlie Lawrence
Age: 10
Lives: Melbourne
Family: Mum, Dad, Aunt Helen, Cooper (cousin), and Rudy (dog)

Hi! I'm Charlie, and this is my school day in Year 4. I wake up at 7:15am and get dressed. In the kitchen, my cousin Cooper is already munching his toast. He and his mum (my aunt, Helen) are staying here until next month when their new house will be ready.

I let my dog Rudy outside and then make toast for me and Aunt Helen.

Australians use British English, so some terms are slightly different. For example:
mum = mom
year = grade
maths = math
pyjamas = pajamas

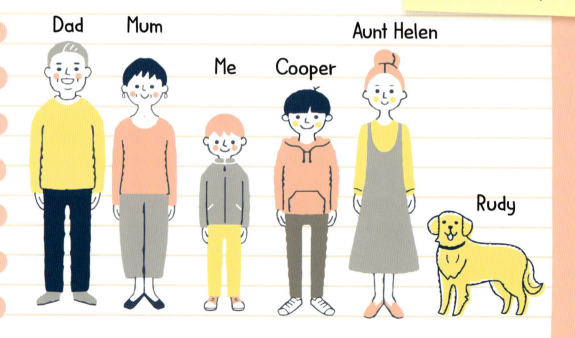

Aunt Helen comes in and helps me make the packed lunches. I say goodbye to my dad when he leaves for work. My mum is a doctor and she's on night shift, so she isn't back yet. I put on my bike helmet, and Aunt Helen, Cooper, and I bike to school.

We get there around 8:40am and I say bye to Aunt Helen. My friends Dessie and Jack are already waiting for me at the bike rails. We go to our classroom as our teacher arrives to take roll call.

Our first class is English. We're learning about adverbs. That's a word that describes how you're doing an action, like, "I'm eating greedily." Next, we have maths. We are studying probability. We get into groups and play a game with dice where we work out the probability of rolling different numbers.

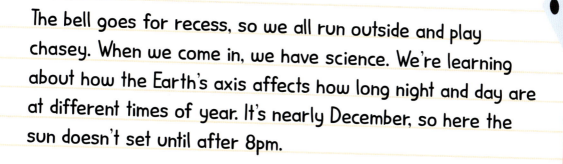

The bell goes for recess, so we all run outside and play chasey. When we come in, we have science. We're learning about how the Earth's axis affects how long night and day are at different times of year. It's nearly December, so here the sun doesn't set until after 8pm.

Chasey: A game of tag.

Next, we have Italian. We go out to the kitchen garden and practice having conversations about things to do with food. It's making me hungry. Luckily, it's now lunchtime!

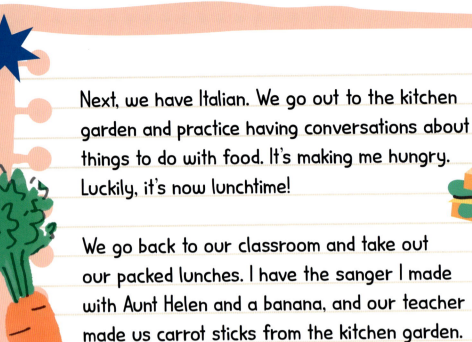

We go back to our classroom and take out our packed lunches. I have the sanger I made with Aunt Helen and a banana, and our teacher made us carrot sticks from the kitchen garden.

Sanger: Australian slang for sandwich.

Kitchen garden: A plot where vegetables and herbs are grown to help students learn about food.

Then we go outside to play handball. There is a grid of four squares painted on the playground and we each go in one square. We hit a tennis ball with our hands so that it bounces into someone else's square. You're out if you hit the ball out of the squares.

After lunch, we have drama. Last week, we worked in groups to make a play from a picture book. We're going to perform them next week, so we rehearse our play. I'm really good at being a mouse!

The bell rings at 3:15pm and we race to the bike rails. I say bye to Jack and Dessie and meet Aunt Helen at the gates. We wait for Cooper, then bike home in the sun.

We're quiet coming in, in case Mum is asleep, but she always gets up around now anyway. I chat with her for a bit, then I have some maths homework to finish. I go out onto the deck and do my homework in the swing chair.

My dad arrives home around 6:20pm and comes with me to take Rudy for a walk. When we get back, Mum and Aunt Helen are making dinner—spag bol—and I help. I've been interested in cooking since we started learning about the kitchen garden. We sit at the table to eat, and I tell everyone about my play at school.

Spag bol: Spaghetti bolognese, a pasta dish with a tomato and meat sauce.

By the time we're done, it's nearly bedtime, so I call Rudy in from the garden and get in my pyjamas. I read for a bit in bed and then call goodnight to everyone. G'night!

 HISTORY

TERRA AUSTRALIS INCOGNITA

People have lived in Australia for more than 60,000 years. They arrived from Asia and Papua New Guinea over land bridges and across small seas. For thousands of years, hundreds of communities lived on the land, each with their own cultures, languages, and techniques of farming, **astronomy**, and **land management.**

Early societies

Early peoples were hunters and gatherers as well as farmers and tool builders. Around the coasts, people farmed crops like yams and grains and dug ditches for fish. Inland communities burned undergrowth to encourage certain plants to grow. Torres Strait Islander peoples were seafarers who fished, farmed, built boats, and navigated by the stars.

 FASCINATING FACT!

Before Europeans ever saw Australia, mapmakers guessed there might be a continent in the Southern Hemisphere. They called it Terra Australis Incognita: "The unknown land of the South."

European arrival

In 1788, the British arrived. They brought prisoners to Australia to work as punishment. This was the start of British **colonization**. At first, the British thought they could take over the land without conflict. But soon, fighting broke out with the Aboriginal peoples who had lived on the land for thousands of years.

A depiction of prisoners arriving in Australia

Forming a country

Gold was discovered in 1851, and people rushed to find their fortune. English **missionaries** arrived in the Torres Strait Islands in 1871 to convert locals to Christianity. In 1901, the colonies joined to form a country. In 1909, the new government began forcibly removing Indigenous children from their families and putting them in white communities as part of a policy called **assimilation**.

Mining for gold

Reversing laws

In 1969, the law allowing Aboriginal children to be taken away was finally removed. In 1973, non-Europeans were allowed to immigrate to Australia for the first time in 70 years. The government began to recognize Indigenous rights to land in 1992, after Eddie Mabo of the Meriam people fought and won a long court case.

Twenty-first century

Today, Australia is a major world economy. It is led by a **democratically elected government**, meaning the people vote on who will be **prime minister**. Teams exist to help Aboriginal peoples access documents about children who were taken (known as the Stolen Generation) to try to find where they came from.

Sydney

THE MAN FROM SNOWY RIVER

Old man Harrison gathered his riders.

"Alright, gents. Settle down. You know why we're here."

The colt from my prize-winning horse Old Regret has run off and joined a herd of brumbies.

"If that herd reaches the mountain, we're in trouble. No horse or rider can get down the other side."

"So who's with me?"

"yeah"

"I'm in"

"yes"

"yes"

But they all laughed at the man from Snowy River and his tiny Timor pony.

"He'll be right, Harrison. That man and pony are from the mountains, we may need them. Just look at his fiery eyes."

"I don't think so, mate. Those hills are far too rough for such as you. And your *pony*."

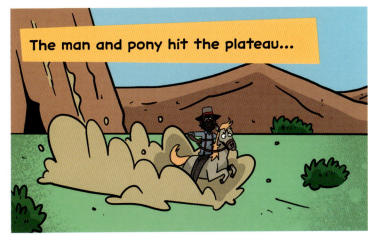

VOCABULARY BUILDER

SAVING THE KOALAS

Bushfires are a risk in Australia, as hot weather and drought mean fire can spread quickly through dry vegetation. Bushfires affect millions of animals, including many koalas. Read this account of a volunteer at a koala sanctuary that takes care of koalas rescued from fires.

Koala

MY LIFE AS A KOALA SANCTUARY VOLUNTEER

After a fire, we get all sorts: orphaned babies, elderly koalas, mothers with their young, and even healthy koalas with nowhere to go. Some have burns and smoke damage. Some have been hit by vehicles or have other injuries. Many are dehydrated or blinded by disease. We take care of them all.

Every day, I prepare the food and clean their dishes. I also help repair and clean out their enclosures. We monitor their health constantly, and I bring them to the vet for treatments. I sometimes go out on rescue calls and give emergency medical treatment, too. If they are injured, we make beds for them out of towels and blankets donated by people. It's great to see how many people care. Part of my job is helping to raise funds for the sanctuary.

Our hope is that we can release them all back into the wild. Last week, we released three healthy koalas, including a joey—a baby koala. I love my job. It is always heartwarming to help **rehabilitate** these wonderful animals.

Koala being fed

What do the volunteers do?
care, clean, feed, fundraise, make beds, monitor, prepare, rehabilitate, release, repair, rescue, treat

Firefighters putting out a bushfire

What are the threats?
blindness, burns, bushfires, dehydration, disease, habitat loss, injury, smoke damage, starvation, vehicles

Imagine you are a volunteer at an animal sanctuary. Describe your day-to-day duties. Think about:
- What kind of animal are you caring for?
- What are the threats to that animal?
- What special care do they need?

GLOSSARY

Agriculture The practice of farming.

Amphibian A cold-blooded animal that can live both in and out of water, such as a frog or newt.

Ancestor A person you are related to who lived a long time ago.

Arid Dry and barren and getting little rain.

Assimilation A policy that attempts to absorb a minority group into the majority culture, overriding their original culture, language, and ways of life.

Astronomy The study of the planets, stars, and other elements of space.

Belief system A set of ideas, values, and stories that influence the way you live your life.

Bight An open bay formed by a bend in a coastline.

Carnivorous Referring to animals (or plants) that eat only meat.

Colonization The act of taking control of a land and settling by force, often displacing people who already exist there.

Conservation The preservation and protection of animals, habitats, and ecosystems.

Continent One of the seven large land masses of Earth: Africa, North America, South America, Asia, Antarctica, Australia, and Europe.

Country A term used by Aboriginal peoples to mean the lands, ecosystems, and waterways they are connected to, physically, spiritually, and ancestrally.

Crustacean A spineless aquatic creature that usually has a hard shell, such as a lobster or shrimp.

Deforestation Clearing of forested areas.

Democratically elected government A government voted in by the people.

Endemic Native to a specific area or country and mainly or only found in that area or country.

Equator An imaginary line around the Earth that is exactly in the middle.

Hemisphere Regions north or south of the equator. There is the Northern Hemisphere and the Southern Hemisphere.

Heritage History, traditions, beliefs, and practices that are inherited from the past.

Indigenous People whose ancestors were the earliest inhabitants of a land or those who inhabited a land before colonists arrived.

Invasive species A non-native species that has been introduced to and colonized an area. They are usually harmful to their environments.

Land management The way in which areas of land are used, developed, and protected using particular techniques.

Mainland The largest part of a country, as opposed to an island.

Missionary A religious person sent to a foreign area to raise awareness of their faith or convert others to their religion.

Monolith A large unbroken piece of stone.

Nation A distinct group of people with its own culture, history, and language. An Indigenous nation might include various clans.

Native Referring to a plant or animal that lives naturally in a place and has not been brought there.

Predator An animal that hunts other animals.

Prime minister The head of an elected government.

Refract To make something like a ray of light or soundwave change direction. Rainbows are caused by refraction and reflection of light.

Rehabilitate To help someone or something get back to good health.

Shrubland A type of land that grows only short, woody plants and grasses.

Soil erosion The loss of the top layer of soil. This results in flooding and poor-quality soil that cannot grow plants well.

Stamen Small stalks at the center of a flower head that produce pollen.

Tectonic activity Movements beneath the Earth's surface. This can result in earthquakes and volcanic eruptions.

Tropical Related to regions around the equator, usually with hot and humid weather all year.

Wildfire A fire that spreads in a natural area such as a forest.

INDEX

A
Aboriginal beliefs 23
Aboriginal culture 6, 18, 19, 23, 25
Aboriginal peoples 6, 10, 11, 18, 19, 23, 37
    see also Anangu Indigenous peoples; Meriam peoples; Torres Strait Islanders
Aboriginal sacred sites 10–11, 23
Anangu 10, 11
Anzac biscuits 24, 28–29
Anzac Day 24, 28
Asian heritage 19, 36
assimilation 37
Australian rules football 21
Australianisms 18, 34, 35
Ayers Rock 11

B
barbecues 20, 24
bats 14
beaches 5, 8, 9, 20, 24
brumbies 38–41
bugs 16
bushfires 42, 43
    see also wildfires

C
Canberra 4, 6, 7, 24, 25
carnivores 13, 14
cassowaries 14
chicken parmi 27
Chinese community 18
Christianity 22–23, 24, 37
Christmas 24
climate change 8, 11
coasts 5, 8, 9, 26, 30, 36
colonization 37
continent 4, 7, 36
coral reefs 8, 9
cricket 21
culture 6, 18–21, 25, 36

D
deforestation 17
deserts 8, 9, 10, 24, 25
dhari 6
didgeridoo 19
Dingo Fence 5
dingoes 5, 13, 16
down under 4
Dreaming, the 23
drinks 27

E
education 31
employment 31
emus 16
endangered species 17
endemic wildlife 12–17
environmental damage 17
    see also bushfires; wildfires
eucalyptus 13, 14, 17
European influences 17, 18, 23, 26
exports 6

F
farming 31, 36
fauna 8, 9, 12–17
flags 6
flora 13, 14, 16, 25
Floriade 25
flying foxes 14
food 16, 26–29
forests 13, 14, 17
    see also rainforests

G
giant clams 15
gold 6, 31, 37
golden wattle 6, 16
Gosse, William 11
government 7, 37
Great Artesian Basin 9
Great Australian Bight 5, 9
Great Barrier Reef 5, 8
greater gliders 17
Griffin, Marion Mahony and Walter Burley 7

H
healthcare 31
history 36–37
houses 30

I
Indigenous peoples 6, 14, 18, 19, 30, 36, 37
    see also Aboriginal peoples; Anangu; Meriam peoples; Torres Strait Islanders

46

Indigenous rights 11, 37
industries 31
insects 16
invasive species 17
iron 9, 31

J
jellyfish 15

K
kangaroos 12
Karlu Karlu 23
koalas 13, 42–43
kookaburras 14

L
land-clearing 17
languages 6, 18

M
Mabo, Eddie 37
mainland 13, 19
Mandarin 18
mantis shrimp 15
marsupials 12–13, 17
meat pie 26
Melbourne 25
Meriam peoples 37
mining 31, 37
missionaries 37
Moomba festival 25

N
national park 10–11
New Zealand 7, 24, 27

O
Oceania 7
ochre 6, 19
opals 6, 7, 31
outback, the 4, 9, 16, 30
outdoor pursuits 20

P
Papua New Guinea 19, 36
Parliament House 7
parrotfish 9
Parrtjima 25
pavlova 27
platypuses 15
Polynesia 7
population 6, 30
public holidays 24

R
rabbits 5, 17
rainforests 8, 9
regent honeyeaters 17
regional days 24
religion 22–23

S
sandstone 11
schools 31
smashed avo 27
sodas 27
soil erosion 17
Southern Hemisphere 4, 36
sports 21, 24
surfing 20
sweet treats 27

T
Tagai 23
Tasmania 4, 13, 24
Tasmanian devils 13
tectonic activity 11
tennis 21
Terra Australis Incognita 36
terrains 8–9
Torres Strait Islanders 4, 6, 19, 22, 23, 36, 37

U
Uluru 5, 10–11

W
wildfires 11, 17
wombats 13
work 31

ACKNOWLEDGMENTS

The publisher would like to thank the following for their kind permission to reproduce their photographs:

(Key: a-above; b-below/bottom; c-center; f-far; l-left; r-right; t-top)

Adobe Stock: Irina 27clb, Jakub 14bl, Joyce 27br, Macronatura.es 16bc (Wolf Spider), New Africa 23cl, Hisa-Nishiya 32br, 33tr, 34bl, 35bl, Alexandre Rosa 7, Sara 11br, Jorge Urraca 27cla, vvoe 7tr; **Alamy Stock Photo:** AAP Image / Ellen Smith 25bl, Martin Berry 30, Lakeview Images 37cra, Bruce Miller 31bl, Minden Pictures / BIA / Jan Wegener 17br, Minden Pictures / Martin Willis 17bl, Universal Images Group North America LLC / Planet Observer 19b; **Depositphotos Inc:** Fotosedrik 43c, Lenanayashkova 35cr, Unnaugan 23bl; **Dreamstime.com:** Rafael Ben Ari 21tr, Supoj Buranaprapapong 19cla, Eduardo Cabanas 15cla, Richie Chan 22, Nataliia Darmoroz 28cb, Peter Hermes Furian 32cla, 33b, 35crb, 43crb, Peter Kolejak 42cr, Tetiana Kovalenko 19tr, Anna Kraynova 6, Robyn Mackenzie 26cra, Irina Miroshnichenko 27bl, Moonkin 27bc (Caramel slice), Mozart3737 37crb, Trung Nguyen 18, Veronika Oliinyk 28tc, 28bl, 28br, Showvector 28bc, Wirestock 13br, Natalia Mishintseva 34tr; **Getty Images:** FIFA / Alex Pantling 6bc, Moment / Belinda Howell 20tr; **Getty Images / iStock:** 11Audrey11 28tr, Uwe-Bergwitz 16bc, DigitalVision / Ezra Shaw 21cla, DMV Photography 16br, Fogaas 24, Isoon Kawsuk 28bc (Coconut), Leamus 13t, Lvinst 27cl, m-e-l 5c, Mladenovic 26crb, Ninikas 29cra, Hisa Nishiya 34cla, PaleStudio 33cr (crb), Hanna Perelygina 31clb (x3), Seraphic06 16crb, Ivan Shchytko 28cl, Rozita Turut 27tl; **Shutterstock.com:** Alexandre.ROSA 8, Anjahennern 9cra, Aratehortua 31tr, AustralianCamera 11cl, Chris Andrews Fern Bay 5tl, Brayden Stanford Photo 13bl, Karen Brough 12, ChameleonsEye 36, Jesus Cobaleda 15bl, Neale Cousland 21br, D.Cunningham 17t, DMV Photography 16bl, Kai Egan 15clb, FiledIMAGE 20br, Fotologer 9tr, Becauz Gao 9cr, Ken Griffiths 14clb, Paul Harding OO 37br, Graphico Imaginarea 29bl, Tim Jessup 9br, Jing S 14cla, JuliusRS 25br, LifeCollectionPhotography 16cr, Anna LoFi 16tr, Milano M 4bl, Millenius 6cb, Holly_Molly 4c, Hisa_Nishiya 32b, Brittany North 23tl, Bhaveshkumar Panchal 43cla, Pattypat 25t, Sham Clicks 20cl, SouthWestImagesAus 10, Surajkalangada 27bc, Thomas Woolsey 14tl, Worldswildlifewonders 15tl

Cover images: *front:* **Adobe Stock:** Red Monkey br; **Dreamstime.com:** Alyssand cr; **Getty Images / iStock:** Nirut Punshiri t; **Shutterstock.com:** Jeep2499 bl; *Back:* **Alamy Stock Photo:** Minden Pictures / BIA / Jan Wegener cl; **Shutterstock.com:** Alexandre.ROSA tl, JuliusRS bl

All of the books in the *DK Super World* series have been reviewed by authenticity readers of the cultures represented to make sure they are culturally accurate.

Aboriginal and Torres Strait Islander readers should be aware that this book may contain names and images of deceased persons.